DINOSAURS
and beasts of yore

GW00891021

DINOSAURS
and beasts of yore

Verses selected by William Cole
Illustrated by Susanna Natti

COLLINS
Cleveland · New York · London

Copyright © 1979 by William Cole.
Illustrations copyright © 1979 by William Collins Publisher Inc.
All rights reserved.
Printed in the United States of America.
Published simultaneously in 1979 by
William Collins Publishers Inc., New York and Cleveland
and William Collins Sons & Company, Ltd., London, Sydney and Glasgow.

Library of Congress Cataloging in Publication Data

Main entry under title: Dinosaurs and beasts of yore.
Summary: A collection of humorous poetry about extinct animals.
1. Extinct animals—Juvenile poetry. 2. Dinosauria—Juvenile
poetry. 3. Children's poetry, American. 4. Children's poetry,
English. 5. Children's poetry, Canadian. [1. Dinosaurs—Poetry.
2. Extinct animals—Poetry. 3. Humorous poetry. 4. Poetry—
Collections] I. Cole, William, 1919-   II. Natti, Susanna.
PS595.E93D5   821'.9'1408   78-31619
ISBN 0-529-05511-2   U.K. ISBN 0-00-195535-7

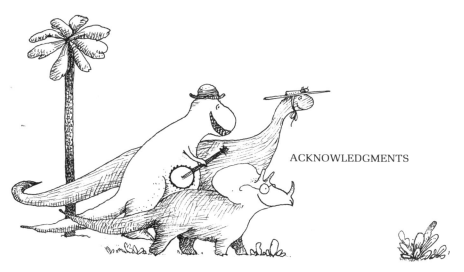

ACKNOWLEDGMENTS

William Collins Publishers, Inc., would like to thank the following authors, publishers, and agents whose interest, cooperation, and permission to reprint have made possible the preparation of *Dinosaurs and Beasts of Yore*. All possible care has been taken to trace the ownership of every selection included and to make full acknowledgment for its use. If any errors have accidentally occurred, they will be corrected in subsequent editions, provided notification is sent to the publishers.

"The Dinosaurs' Dinner" by Dennis Lee from *Alligator Pie Calendar* by Dennis Lee and Frank Newfield. Reprinted by permission of The Macmillan Company of Canada, Ltd.

"My Dinosaur's Day in the Park" by Elizabeth Winthrop. Copyright © 1979 by Elizabeth Winthrop Mahony. Reprinted by permission of the author.

"The Largest of Them All" and "No Accounting for Tastes" by J. A. Lindon. Reprinted by permission of the author.

"Brachiosaurus" by Mary Ann Hoberman. Copyright © 1979 by Mary Ann Hoberman. Reprinted by permission of Russell & Volkening, Inc., as agents for the author.

"If I Had a Brontosaurus" from *Where the Sidewalk Ends* by Shel Silverstein. Copyright © 1974 by Shel Silverstein. Reprinted by permission of Harper & Row, Publishers, Inc.

"The Tyrannosaurus Rex" and "If You Pinch a Dinosaur" by Shel Silverstein. Reprinted by permission of the author.

"Long Gone" from *A Gopher in the Garden and Other Animal Poems* by Jack Prelutsky. Copyright © 1966, 1967 by Jack Prelutsky. Reprinted by permission of Macmillan Publishing Co., Inc.

"The Dinosaur" from *It Takes a Lot of Paper to Gift-Wrap an Elephant* by Louis Phillips. Copyright © 1973 by Louis Phillips. Reprinted by permission of the author and Prologue Press.

"Abiding Question" by Steven Kroll. Copyright © 1979 by Steven Kroll. Reprinted by permission of Joan Daves, as agent for the author.

"The Mastodon" and "The Tyrannosaur" by Michael Braude. Reprinted by permission of the author.

"The Brontosaurus" and "The Pterodactyl" by H.A.C. Evans. Reprinted by permission of the author.

"Dinosaurs" from *More Small Poems* by Valerie Worth. Poems copyright © 1976 by Valerie Worth. Reprinted by permission of Farrar, Straus & Giroux, Inc., and Curtis Brown, Ltd.

"To the Skeleton of a Dinosaur in the Museum" by Lilian Moore. Reprinted by permission of the author.

"Company" from *Upside Down and Inside Out: Poems For All Your Pockets* by Bobbi Katz. Copyright © 1973 by Bobbi Katz. Reprinted by permission of Franklin Watts, Inc.

"The Dinosaur" by Edward Lucie-Smith. Copyright © 1976 by Edward Lucie-Smith.

"Here He Comes" by Marnie Pomeroy. Reprinted by permission of the author. "Time Zones" from *Who Would Marry a Mineral?* by Lillian Morrison. Copyright © 1978 by Lillian Morrison. Reprinted by permission of Lothrop, Lee & Shepard Co. (A division of William Morrow & Co.)

"Lines on a Small Potato" by Margaret Fishback. Copyright © 1963 by Margaret Fishback Antolini. Reprinted by permission of the author.

"The Trouble with a Dinosaur" from *One Winter Night in August and Other Nonsense Jingles* by X. J. Kennedy (A Margaret K. McElderry Book). Copyright © 1975 by X. J. Kennedy. "Dinosaur Din" and "Tyrannosaurus Rex's Teeth" from *The Phantom Ice Cream Man* by X. J. Kennedy (A Margaret K. McElderry Book). Copyright © 1979 by X. J. Kennedy. Reprinted by permission of Atheneum Publishers and Curtis Brown, Ltd.

"I Spy Tyrannosaurus" by Pyke Johnson, Jr. Reprinted by permission of the author.

"The Pterodactyl" by André Moul Ross. Copyright © 1979 by André Moul Ross. Reprinted by permission of the author.

The reader will find both British and
American spellings in the poems in this book.
The publisher has chosen to retain
the original spellings throughout.

Contents

So It Goes

In days of yore the dinosaur
Tromped about the forest floor.

He watched the pterodactyl fly
Across the prehistoric sky;

The ichthyosaurus—he was docile—
Is now extinct, or is a fossil.

And in another million years,
Like these, *we'll* be extinct, my dears!

William Cole

Not Me!

The iguanodon looked like our iguana;
Would you like to pet one? *I* don't wanna!

William Cole

The Tyrannosaur

Tyrannosaur remains are found
most anywhere above the ground:
the reason, it can be presumed,
they were too big to be entombed.

Michael Braude

The Dinosaurs' Dinner

Allosaurus, stegosaurus,
Brontosaurus too,
All went off for dinner at the
Dinosaur zoo;

Along came the waiter, called
Tyrannosaurus Rex,
Gobbled up the table
'Cause they wouldn't pay their checks.

Dennis Lee

15

Dinosaur Din

Did stegosaurus bellow like
A longhorn steer in Texas?
Could a songbird's tweet
Or twitter beat
Tyrannosaurus Rex's?

Did pterodactyl cackle?
Did brachiosaurus bray?
Did monoclonius toot
Through his horny snoot
Ta ra ra boom de ay?

Did little lambeosaurus baa
Or did it bark in chorus?
Did the ankles clank
Like an army tank
On an ankylosaurus?

Today cars, planes and subway trains
Raise a whole lot of hullaballoo
But the rumble and roar
Of a dinosaur
I haven't once heard—have you?

                              X. J. Kennedy

The Eohippus

The Eohippus
Was a horse so small
He'd trippus.

William Cole

To the Skeleton of a Dinosaur in the Museum

Hey there, Brontosaurus!
You were here so long before us
Your deeds can never bore us.
How *were* the good old days?

Did you really like to graze?
Did you often munch
With a prehistoric crunch
On a giant tree—or two—or three
For lunch?

As you went yon and hither
Were you ever in a dither
When your head and distant tail
Went different ways?

Did you shake the earth like thunder
With your roars and groans?
I wonder . . . . . . Say, it's hard
To have a conversation
With your bones.

Lilian Moore

If I Had a Brontosaurus

If I had a brontosaurus,
I would name him Horace or Morris.
But if suddenly one day he had
A lot of little brontosauri—
I would change his name
To Laurie.

Shel Silverstein

Company

I'm fixing a lunch for a dinosaur.
Who knows when one might come by?
I'm pulling up all the weeds I can find.
I'm piling them high as the sky.
I'm fixing a lunch for a dinosaur.
I hope he will stop by soon.
Maybe he'll just walk down my street
And have some lunch at noon.

Bobbi Katz

The Dinosaur

The dinosaur had two brains.
One in his head
& one in his tail,
So how did he fail?

Well,
Let me put a bee in your bonnet—
If you have a good brain,
Don't sit on it.

Louis Phillips

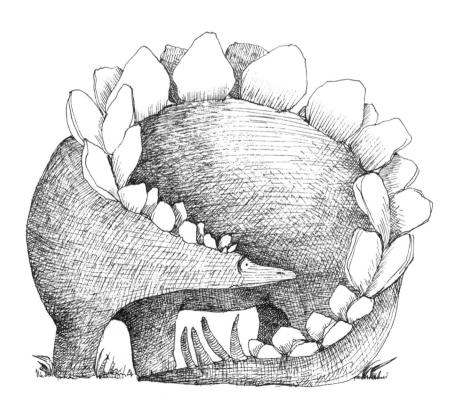

Time Zones

As I was cruising through the galaxies
Floating on a solar breeze
A giant egg came swirling by.
"Where to, enormous egg?" sang I.

It answered in a rush of air
"I do not know, nor do I care,
And I certainly won't be back till
I've delivered this pterodactyl."

Lilian Morrison

It's All Relative

"My! You're a tiny little runt!"
Said the dinosaur to the elephant.

William Cole

My Dinosaur's Day in the Park

My pet dinosaur got in trouble
When we went for a walk in the park.
I took off his leash and let him run free.
He didn't come back until dark.

He ate up the new row of oak trees
(The gardener was fit to be tied).
Then he stopped in the playground and bent down his head
And the kids used his neck for a slide.

He knocked down the fence by the boat pond
With a swing of his twenty-foot tail;
When he stopped to explain he was sorry,
His legs blocked the bicycle trail.

When the sun set, my dino got worried;
He's always been scared of the dark.
He sat down on the ground and started to cry.
His tears flooded out the whole park.

A friend of mine rowed his boat over
When he heard my pet dino's sad roar.
He showed him the way home to my house
And helped him unlock the front door.

He's a lovable, lumbering fellow
But after my pet had his spree,
They put up a sign in the park and it reads,
NO DINOS ALLOWED TO RUN FREE.

Elizabeth Winthrop

Brachiosaurus

This dinosaur is now extinct
While I am still extant.
I'd like to bring it back alive.
                        (Unhappily, I can't.)

The largest ones weighed fifty tons
And stood three stories high.
Their dinner ration? Vegetation.
                        (Never hurt a fly.)

Alas! Alack! They're dead and gone
Through failure to adapt
And only known by track and bone.
                        (I wish we'd overlapped.)

                        Mary Ann Hoberman

Dudley Not Cuddly

I had a wooly mammoth pet,
I named him Little Dudley;
I finally had to let him go,
'Cause he wasn't very cuddly.

William Cole

Here He Comes

Here he comes,
the grey-green weirdo bumbling along,
covered with scales and horns.

Here he is,
his head bobbing in clouds with a pea-sized thought
for all his mountains of size.

There he goes,
his feet like grey-green bulldozers
with treetops caught between his toes.

Marnie Pomeroy

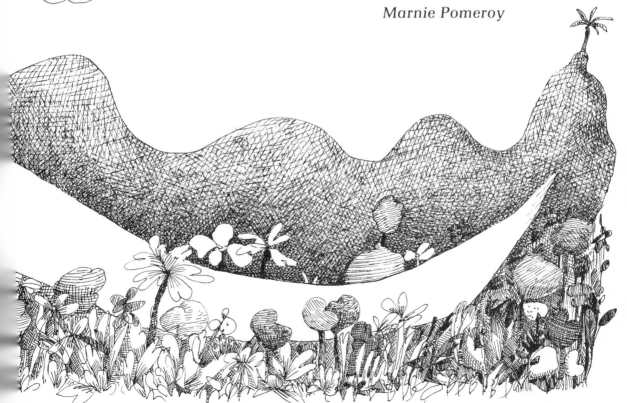

Night Voyage

One night I couldn't fall asleep
and while I lay there, counting sheep,
my mother came and read to me
about the world that used to be.
But—honest—I was sound awake
when I set sail upon the lake.

I landed on a far-off shore
and there I met a dinosaur
three quarters of a mountain high.
Its head reached nearly to the sky.
It had a tail two rivers long.
I said, "There must be something wrong.
One doesn't sail to far-off shores
in hope of meeting dinosaurs.
I'd rather meet Pinocchio."
The creature raged and snorted so
it shriveled all the grass and trees
and shook the mountains to their knees.
The air had turned an awful blue.
I said, "Oh, what am I to do?"
There stood a tree all blanched and withered.
It whispered, "Thither!"
                              and I thithered.

                    —Mildred Luton

The Pterodactyl

Long ago the pterodactyl
Through the air was wont to flit,
And continued so to act till
Evolution finished it.

H. A. C. Evans

34

Lines on a Small Potato

Reflect upon the dinosaur,
A giant that exists no more.
Though brawny when he was alive,
He didn't manage to survive,
Whereas the unimpressive flea
Continues healthy as can be;
So do not whimper that you're small—
Be happy that you're here at all.

Margaret Fishback

Take My Advice

The diplodocus weighed twenty ton;
In every battle—guess who won?
(If you should ever meet one—RUN!)

William Cole

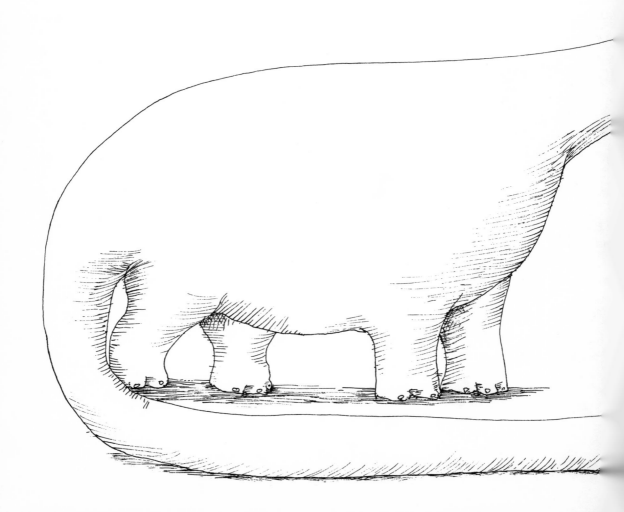

The Mastodon

The mastodon
has traveled on
his only trace
a skeleton.

The north of Asia
his habitat;
then came the glacier
and that was that.

Michael Braude

I Spy Tyrannosaurus

When active dinosaur children
   Used to play "Blind Dinosaur's Bluff,"
They found that being bumped into
   Could be exceedingly rough.
So blindfolded dinosaur players
   Would have other dinosaurs guide them;
But they never played "Hide and Go Seek"—
   There was no place big enough to hide them.

Pyke Johnson, Jr.

Abiding Question

My
stegosaur
snores.
Does
yours?

Steven Kroll

Long Gone

Don't waste your time in looking for
the long-extinct tyrannosaur,
because this ancient dinosaur
just can't be found here anymore.

This also goes for stegosaurus,
allosaurus, brontosaurus
and any other kind of saurus.
They all lived here before us.

Jack Prelutsky

S'no Fun

"Dinosaur" means "terrible lizard"—
I'd hate to meet one in a blizzard.

William Cole

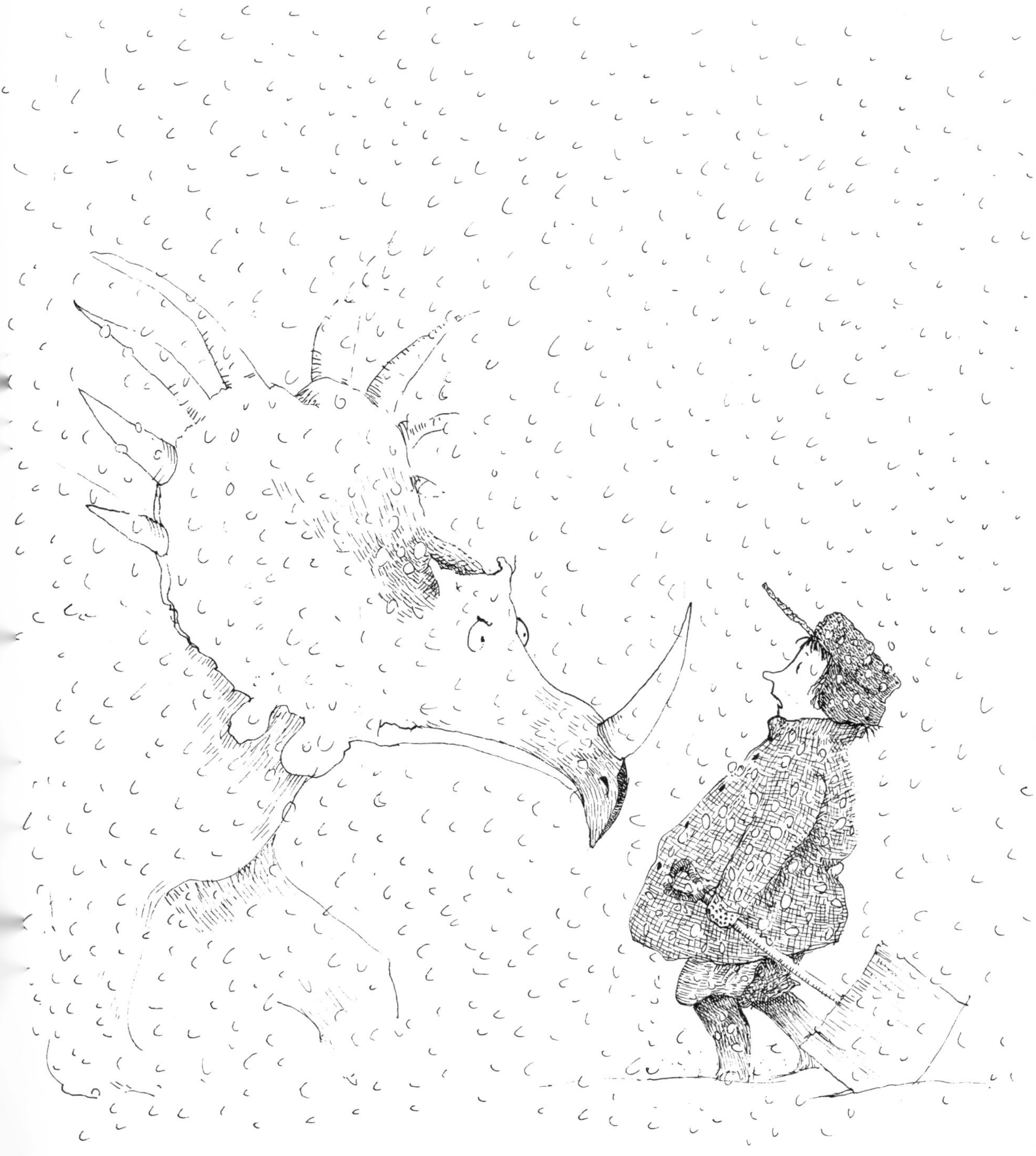

The Brontosaurus

The brontosaurus ranged the earth
   Ten million years ago;
He was a beast of monstrous girth
   But very, very slow.

His neck was long, his tail was too,
   His head was very small;
His length (all this, you know, is true)
   Was sixty feet in all.

And everybody that he met
   He used to terrify
He was so big and ugly, yet
   He wouldn't hurt a fly.

He was a lizard-type, I'm told;
   Ate seaweed, so they say,
Inspiring us, both young and old
   To eat our greens each day.

H. A. C. Evans

The Pterodactyl

A pterodactyl drove his Edsel
  Down a busy street.
"There's nothing really wrong," he said,
  "With being obsolete!"

André Moul Ross

The Trouble with a Dinosaur

The trouble with a dinosaur
Is how to move while ambling
And how to sit and hatch her eggs
Without the whole bunch scrambling.

X. J. Kennedy

No Accounting for Tastes

The iguanodon
Today is gone,
She never knew or met us;
She fed on plants
Like many aunts,
Who seem to thrive on lettuce.

The allosaurus
Lived before us
Likewise—not on plants.
The allosaurus
Leapt and tore us—
He fed upon the aunts!

J. A. Lindon

I'm Scared

The pterodactyl's mildness has never been verified.
So the pterodactyl, to tell the truth, has me pterrified.

William Cole

The Dinosaur

This poem is too small, I fear,
  To hold a dinosaur.
I led him here, but he was there,
  And there was always more.

How can I hope to fit the beast
Within this cage of metre?
He's sixty fathoms long, at least—
A hamster would be neater.

Edward Lucie-Smith

Tyrannosaurus Rex's Teeth

Tyrannosaurus Rex's teeth
Were pearly-white and porous.
To file their points
He'd chomp on joints
Of pachycephalosaurus.

"Why, Ty, your teeth are total wrecks!
They'll need a ton of drilling!"—
Ty opened wide
And Doc McBride
Supplied him with a filling.

X. J. Kennedy

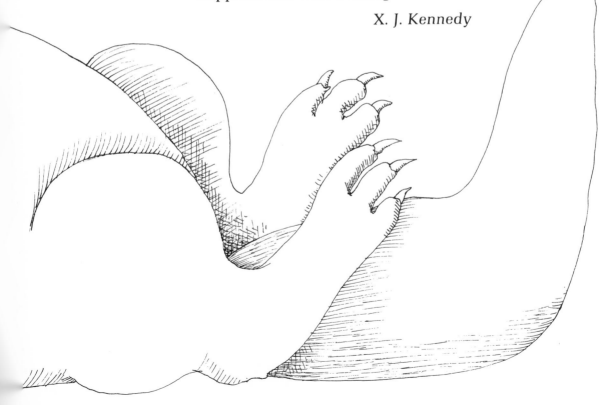

Better Than a Pussycat?

The pteranodon was a flying snake—
What a lovely pet he'd make!

William Cole

Dinosaurs

Dinosaurs
Do not count,
Because
They are all
Dead:

None of us
Saw them, dogs
Do not even
Know that
They were there—

But they
Still walk
About heavily
In everybody's
Head.

Valerie Worth

If You Pinch a Dinosaur

If you pinch a Dinosaur
You might get him kinda sore;
He might bite and he might roar!
Better pinch the kid next door.

Shel Silverstein

May Be

There are no more monsters, I have to confess—
Except that there *may* be deep under Loch Ness!

William Cole

The Tyrannosaurus Rex

The Tyrannosaurus Rex
Had twenty-four-foot necks;
They'd gobble you up in a wink.
How nice that they're extinct.

Shel Silverstein

The Largest of Them All

Eighty feet long was the brachiosaur,
   And her weight was fifty tons!
I can't think what I'd use her for,
If anyone gave me a brachiosaur;
She wouldn't go in or go out of the door,
   And she'd gobble up scores of buns;
And, really, there isn't room on the floor
For even a curled-up brachiosaur.

And another thing one can't ignore,
   She might have daughters and sons.
My Dad and Mom might well get sore,
Overrun by brachiosaurs galore,
Who'd grunt and rumble and cough and roar
   With a noise like distant guns.
Enough, enough, we'll say no more—
As a pet, forget the brachiosaur!

J. A. Lindon

The Only Place

The dinosaurs are gone—where can you see 'em?
In the museum.

William Cole